BRITAIN IN OLD PHOTOGRAPHS

COLCHESTER
1940–1990

A CHANGING TOWN

ANDREW PHILLIPS

SUTTON PUBLISHING LIMITED

Sutton Publishing Limited
Phoenix Mill · Thrupp · Stroud
Gloucestershire · GL5 2BU

First published 1996
Reprinted with corrections 1996
Reprinted 1998

Cover photographs: *front*: construction of the
BT tower; *back*: a VE day street party at
Wickham Road.

British Library Cataloguing in Publication Data
A catalogue record for this book is available from the
British Library.

ISBN 0-7509-1301-0

Typeset in 10/12 Perpetua.
Typesetting and origination by
Sutton Publishing Limited.
Printed in Great Britain by
Ebenezer Baylis, Worcester

A quiet moment in St Nicholas Street in the 1950s with Kent & Blaxill's shop on the left. The Cross Keys
pub has not yet been demolished or Wyre Street pedestrianized. (62B)

CONTENTS

The top of Balkerne Hill as it appeared before the inner ring road was built in 1976.

High Street, *c.* 1960. The Cups Hotel (right) at this time is still a flourishing concern, and Williams and Griffins have not yet amalgamated. Cars park where they please, for as long as they please; but then, most people don't have cars.

INTRODUCTION

This is the sequel to my previous book, *Colchester in Old Photographs*, and although that ends in 1955, I have tried to avoid duplication. The Second World War, for example, is most fully covered there. Here I have tried to chart fifty years of change in Colchester's appearance; fifty years in which more has been added and changed than in the previous history of the whole town.

On the surface, much of 1940s Colchester can still be seen, providing a book of photographs with lots of contrast between 'then and now'. Old firms still trade: Paxmans, Woods, BT, Colchester Co-op; old institutions still flourish: the Oyster Feast, the Carnival, Rotary, the U's and civic ritual has survived local government reorganization and all the attacks of the 'angry brigade'. Above all, there has evolved a sympathetic awareness of townscape heritage. The High Street has been set in aspic, so to speak, with original or replica Victorian façades pasted on to the steel and concrete buildings that lay behind them.

Meanwhile the population has doubled and the town centre become choked with traffic. Something had to give. What Hitler had spared fell foul of modern retailing. Scores of little shops and houses, often red-roofed, traditional buildings, gave way to warehouse superstores and pedestrianized precincts. From the mid-1960s this became controversial with the rise of the Civic Society and the role of the borough council as a developer. The Lion Walk complex (built between 1972 and 1974) and the Culver Precinct (1987) both cleared large areas of buildings, excavating craters to house pile-driven concrete and create underground service facilities. Rescue archaeology made Colchester one of the best-studied Roman towns in Britain.

The needs of the motor car forced even greater changes. A dual carriageway inner ring road, still unfinished in 1990, demolished much in its path, as Southway and Balkerne Hill (1975/6) linked up with the 1930s bypass – which was, in turn, itself bypassed. Six multi-storey car parks attempted ever more ingenious architecture to disguise their size and weight.

This book therefore focuses on structural change, for time cannot stand still. Economically, from 1940 to 1990, Colchester has been a success story. Shoppers in 1940, lean and wearing hats, could scarcely imagine today's choice. Whether these changes – making an enlarged and diverse Colchester – have spoilt a charming and historic town, is more complex an issue. The photographs, therefore, must speak for themselves, but they are seldom spontaneous or free from social messages. The real authors are the photographers and I have tried to name them all below. I hope, if they are reading this, they will accept this praise. Praise also goes, above all, to Essex County Newspapers and two generations of press photographers. Their archive is unique. So too is our Museum Resource Centre collection. Where would this book be without Horace Poulter's brilliant photographic survey of 1940?

My thanks are also due, alphabetically to avoid distinction, to John Bensusan-Butt, Graham Bober, Jackie Bowis, Norman Catchpole, Crawford Gillan, Marcel Glover, Yana Griffiths, Rona Hammond, Rita Hills, Tom Hodgson, Christine Mabbitt, Keith Mirams, Keith Parker, Bernard Polley, Francis Ponder, Rosanne Pyle, Jim Robinson, Bob Russell, Daphne Woodward and Joan Wright. I have tried to include pictures that reflect significant change; to cover all decades equally; even to have a photo for every year from 1940 to 1990. There was not room for everything – apologies to the Garrison, the Scouts, The Chamber, Colchester Zoo, Essex Cricket Week and suburban Colchester as a whole.

There are bound to be mistakes. If you spot one, or can add to our knowledge, please write and tell us, via: Andrew Phillips, Museum Resources Centre, 14 Ryegate Road, Colchester. And if you have old photographs dating from 1940 to 1990 which you no longer need, please consider sending them to the Museum or to Essex County Newspapers, Oriel House, North Hill, Colchester.

To provide comparisons between photos in this book as well as with those in *Colchester in Old Photographs* I have put page numbers in brackets followed by the letters T or B, meaning top or bottom, after some captions. OP before a number refers to Colchester in Old Photographs. Thus, OP26T means compare this photo with that at the top of page 26 in *Colchester in Old Photographs*. Therefore there are 550 photographs of Colchester for comparative analysis.

Dedication

To all the photographers, including; John Adams, David Barker, Diane Barker, Des Blake-Amos, Steve Brading, Nigel Brown, Eric Cheek, Mike Cleary, Peter Clements, John Clissold, Peter Elinskas, Roy Farthing, Anne Forshaw, Marcel Glover, Dave Higgleton, Laurie Honeyball, David Mansell, Ian Massingham, Keith Mirams, Roy Mullen, Horace Poulter, Adrian Rushden, Greg Szpurko, Roger Tamblyn, Terry Weeden, Ray Wood and Peter Wright.

1940–1959
SOMEWHERE IN
EAST ANGLIA

(the BBC)

The first thirty-seven photos in this section are part of a street-by-street survey completed in 1940. It begins at the top of High Street. (OP 58T)

Three little girls from the Convent school drift down Priory Street, past houses destined to become a car park. Is there really a war on? (64T)

Servicemen stroll along St John's Street. These assorted shops survived Hitler only to be replaced by Centurion House. (73B)

Lots of cycle power at the top of Crouch Street, north side. All these buildings are still there today. (OP 143)

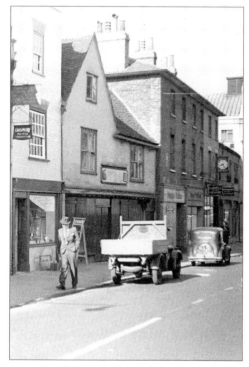

Crouch Street, south side. Left: a fireman cycles past Maldon Road, towards the Red Garage. Right: the view from The Bull to the Regal (now the Odeon). (40T, 57B)

The top of High Street, with St Peter's church tower behind. This building had been a fish shop since at least 1820. Wartime deprivation does not prevent them advertising 'English Duckling' and 'Pure Scottish Salmon'.

High Street, seen from below the Hippodrome, opposite East Stockwell Street. (28B)

Trinity Street before the churchyard railings were removed for the wartime salvage campaign. The buildings on the right now house the new Cups Hotel. (119B)

The Co-op's Colco Corner. One law-abiding gentleman is carrying his gas mask. (47B)

Head Street, west side. The buildings remain much the same today.

A barely recognizable Osborne Street. Note the electricity works in the distance. (68B)

The Head Warden's car is parked in Culver Street just beyond Trinity Street. The building on the left, Trinity Chambers, housed the Clerk to the Justices office.

Culver Street West. Lay & Wheeler's shop looks much as it looked in 1990, but it has rather a different van parked outside. (100T)

The wartime Dutch Quarter: Maidenburgh Street, just above Hope Hall. (OP 137B)

The West Stockwell Street fish shop looks disturbingly empty. The black and white kerb helped cyclists in the blackout.

St Botolph's Street, west side, looking quite busy.

The photographer of this scene has just been spotted by these four shoppers in Long Wyre Street.

High Street below the sandbagged Town Hall. Lampposts and junction boxes are striped white to be seen in the blackout. (28B, OP 101B)

Kent & Blaxill's (left) survived the war but was burnt down afterwards.(35T) Ladies at the corner of Roman Road (right) seem unmoved by the posters. The site still displays posters today.

Rolling out the barrel for the Ship Inn, East Hill. During the First World War beer-drinking had declined in Colchester; during the Second it increased.

Windows in Sir Isaac's Walk taped against bomb blasts; they still survive there today.

Elegant houses in Queen Street west were doomed to destruction after the war. (59B)

The Colchester Brewing Co. on East Hill with its rather token sandbag defence.

Houses stand on the Roman Wall in Vineyard Street; a public shelter sits below.

Horace Poulter of Colchester Museum – who took all these photographs – views a postwar exhibition in the Castle of photos taken by British and American troops.

The morning after the St Botolph's Corner incendiary bombing, 24 February 1944. Above: the Osborne Street/St Botolph's junction, looking towards Mersea Road. (OP 140B) Below: the shell of Hollington's factory damped down in the chill light of dawn by ghostly firemen. (43B, OP 35)

The works' fire brigade at Paxman's Britannia Works in 1944. (OP 141T, 115B)

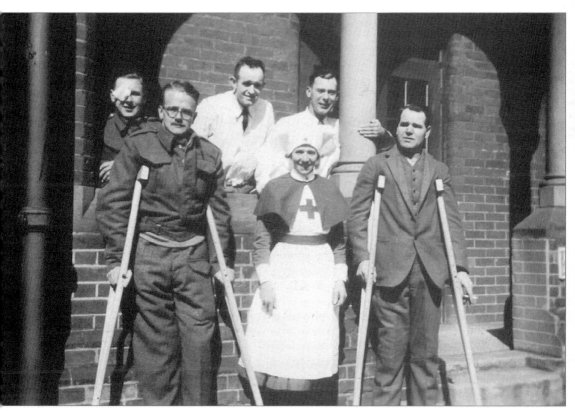

Nurse Norton with the (just) walking wounded at the Military Hospital in 1942.

Evacuees from Wilson Marriage school at Stoke-on-Trent in 1940.

Making uniforms in Crowther's factory brought many older women back into the workforce. (OP 98B)

A Colchester ambulance team in 1941.

Dad's Army: part of the Langham platoon of the Home Guard.

German prisoners mend boots at the Berechurch Hall prisoner of war camp. Later they were often seen working on local farms. (OP 150)

The same camp, thirty years later, serves as a 'glasshouse' for Army offenders. Notorious National Service 'graduates' included the Kray twins.

Workers knocking off from Paxman's main factory on Hythe Hill. Its 1,750-strong workforce was the largest supplier of engines to the Admiralty during the war. (115T, OP 39T)

Workers at St Leonard's Laundry on Hythe Hill enjoy a postwar outing. (58T, OP 128)

Causton Road victory street party, May 1945. Where did they get that cake? (OP 149T)

VE day street party at Wickham Road, one of sixty such celebrations held in Colchester.

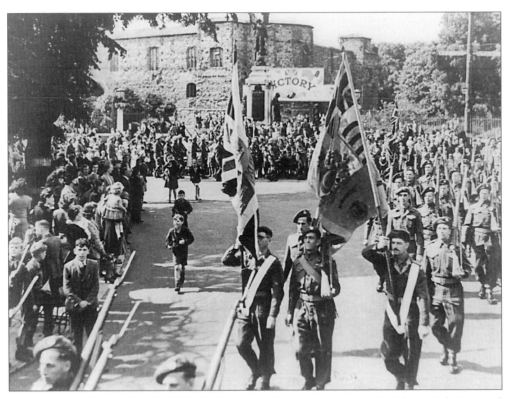

Part of the great Victory Parade of May 1946, when the Essex Regiment marched down High Street and round Queen Street with fixed bayonets. The castle can be seen behind. (OP 147)

A children's fancy dress street party in St Peter's Street, 1945.

Colchester's first roundabout at North Station Road, in the winter of 1945. Essex Hall is on the horizon. (85B,110B,OP 65)

High Street during the same winter. The wartime water storage tank is still beside the Hippodrome. (16T)

Charles Smith (centre), Colchester's first Labour MP, chats to two workmen in 1947 at the new Barn Hall Estate. With him is his agent, Jack Andrews, chairman of the Housing Committee. (30T)

'Prefabs', built as temporary structures on Sussex Road in 1946, survived until the 1970s.

Charles Smith MP, Jack Andrews and site officials pose by the new Orlitt houses built from 'kits' which lie in the foreground, 1947.

Book publisher William Foyle conducts an auction in the Moot Hall in 1948, organized by the Rotary Club to help finance the building of homes for the elderly.

Mayor Leonard Dansie lays the foundation stone of homes for the elderly in Balkerne Gardens, built as a Second World War memorial in 1949. This building programme was part-financed by the Nuffield Foundation. The group on the left includes Frederick Parsley (far left) and Sam Blomfield (wearing a bow tie).

The young find entertainment at the 'pictures' — as here in 1950 at the Hippodrome behind the taxi rank. (28B)

George Strauss, Minister of Labour, gives men at the Britannia Works a 1948 pep-talk on postwar reconstruction; Ted Paxman, top left, leads the applause. (115B)

Loading Spillers animal food for Pertwees at the Hythe in 1958: a mixture of muscle and mechanics that marked the postwar period.

Postwar education fosters democracy: East Ward School pupils visit a war-scarred Parliament with their MP, Charles Smith.

Postwar internationalism: the 1948 inter-town sports contest held with contestants from Zwolle in Holland. The cup presentation ceremony took place in Mayor Dansie's Parlour. (107B)

'Back to normal' included the revival of the Carnival, and this is the Rowhedge Iron Works' Festival of Britain entry, 1951. (99B, OP 124B)

The Oyster Feast was also revived. This is the 1950 feast with Mayor Jack Andrews. (OP 56)

The fire at Kent & Blaxill's in High Street, 1952. George Farmer's old shop was saved but drenched in the process. (OP 68T, OP 46B)

Middle Mill on the river in 1950, by then reduced to a storage depot, fell into a slow decline and was subsequently demolished. (OP 148T)

Painting the floodgates on Hythe Quay after the 1953 floods. The gasworks are still in full operation. (88T)

The Victorian warehouses at the Hythe are still picturesque, but barges are few and far between.

Despite nationalization, the 1956 rail service from North Station did not lose its wartime reputation for unreliability. Nor had the Guinness Book of Records yet credited the station with the longest platform in Britain. (86B)

A 1960 diesel shuttle from St Botolph's Station on the picturesque old line to Brightlingsea. (87T)

Looking up North Hill in 1953: no parking restrictions and no yellow lines.

Road repairs in St John's Street do not cause a traffic jam as they would today. (108B, OP 106B)

The Headgate tobacconist, on the corner of Crouch Street, a traditional timbered building, shortly before it was demolished.

These timbered buildings in Queen Street still survive today. The railings surrounding All Saints' churchyard, removed in the war, are now restored.

The Horse & Groom pub at the junction of Balkerne Hill and Crouch Street was demolished in 1959. (82B)

This 1953 view of Queen Street, above the Short Wyre Street junction, is hard to recall today. (59B)

Old shops: a newsagent, cycle shop and petrol pumps, seen in East Street, in 1955, are soon to be replaced by a modern petrol station and forecourt.

New shops: a 'brown field' site, Queen Elizabeth Way, on the new Monkwick Estate.

The eponymous Prettygate Farm with the original 'pretty gate', which survived until the 1990s, behind the Prettygate pub.

The Commons in 1959, part of the large Prettygate development by Colchester builders, W.A. Hills & Son. (OP 128T)

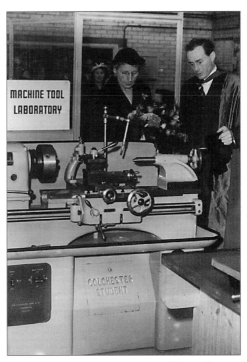

The Technical College at Sheepen Road (left), now part of a large campus, was Colchester's most prestigious new building when it was opened (right) by Minister of Education, Florence Horsbrugh, in 1954, seen with the Principal, Dr Stephens, viewing a new Colchester lathe. (114B, OP 153B)

Another new building replaced Hollington's old factory in 1955 – only to make way for Southway in 1974. (55B)

Griffin's 1955 Head Street furniture store amalgamated with Williams in High Street, making way for Tesco's and later still, for Debenhams. (122T)

Day's Garage managed to adapt the old 'Port Reeve's House' on the East Bay and Brook Street junction where they had traded for forty years. (OP 26T)

Mr Gosling's Red Garage had, by 1955, been a Crouch Street landmark for fifty years. (9B, OP 105T)

Cars are beginning to sell well as Adams open their new Culver Street showroom in 1955. (OP 104B)

Sir Mortimer Wheeler entertains Mayor Charles Lee and the Essex Archaeological Society at their 1952 centenary banquet in the Moot Hall. Bishop Narborough smokes a medieval cigarette.

Coronation street party, Harsnett Road, 1953. Would you mistake it for 1945? (26)

Left: the 1953 Coronation arch across East Hill frames the spire of St Nicholas. (49) Right: bunting in Pelham's Lane during a Tattoo Week in 1973. (121, OP 93T)

The 1953 Coronation display at the Co-op's Colco Corner. (11B)

Jumbo the water-tower is lit up for the Coronation. Its traditional tiled roof is not yet copper-topped.

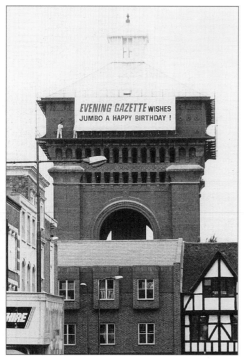
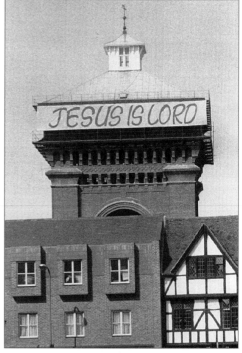

Jumbo the ultimate billboard. In 1983 on its centenary (left) and as a prayer tower for Christian evangelicals in 1989 (right).

The demolition of Sir George Gilbert Scott's Victorian-Gothic St Nicholas Church in 1955. No proper record was made of this fine building and historic site. Shoppers shuffle past the billboards. (OP 159)

The flattened St Nicholas Church site in 1956. Across the road, on the corner of Maidenburg Street, Joslin's the ironmongers will soon be flattened too. In the process John Joslin's historic photographic collection was destroyed. (OP 9)

The Co-op's St Nicholas House was newly finished in 1957.

Opening Day at St Nicholas House, 1957. Crowds (above) queue for the wonder of the age, defiant TVs, and (below) try the new Silver Seal margarine. (61)

Lexden Manor, home of David Papillon (seen top left at the microphone), plays host to a 1950s garden party, possibly on behalf of the Conservative Party.

Old houses in East Street, 1955: picturesque but decrepit.

A Drury Farm Dairy milk float, pulled by Judy the horse, outside Castle Gates in 1956.

Two-way traffic in the High Street: a photograph dedicated to all survivors of 1950s rain-proof plastic macs.

From 1940 (above) to 1955 (below) the pace in Head Street and the use of its buildings did not greatly change. (OP 96T) In the next twenty years, however, the volume of traffic would.

1960–1976

THE PRICE
OF PROGRESS

(Essex County Standard)

From the air, Southway, linked by the St Botolph's and Maldon Road roundabouts, cuts a swathe through the town in 1975.

High Street, east, from the top of the town hall in 1964. The new steel and concrete Woolworths, up from St Nicholas House which housed the Co-op, thrusts above the pitched roofs of the Red Lion.

The new Woolworths from ground level in 1964.

A quiet Crouch Street in 1960. The buildings on the right were demolished to make way for the Maldon Road roundabout. (9B)

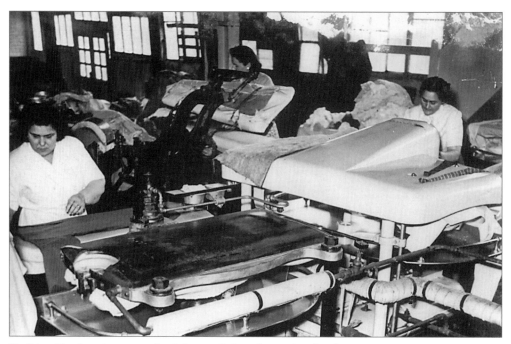

Traditional hard work continued at St Leonard's Laundry until it closed in 1959.

The office at the Repertory Theatre in 1967, perhaps typical of many small offices of this date. From left to right, June Cullum, David Forder, John Alder and Olga Richards. (91B)

The old Queen Street/Wyre Street Arcade (left) was replaced by the concrete Kingsway (now Priory Walk) in 1969 (right).

The bridge over Queen Street, built in 1972, enabled motorists to walk directly into Keddie's modern store. (40B, 77T)

Retail revolution: seconds before the opening of Sainsbury's Kingsway store, their second largest in Britain, in 1969. Acres of shelving (below) were still a novelty then.

The Co-op's first attempt at self-service (left) needed some explaining. Traditional greengrocers in Maldon Road, 1971, (right) were demolished by the building of the Southway. (55)

The growth of a legend: Gunton's extend their delicatessen grocery in 1960.

A traffic jam in Crouch Street outside new Gunton's in 1968. The buildings on the left were demolished to make way for the dual carriageway.

The Co-op (left) colonizes Wyre Street. All these buildings were replaced by 1970. Christmas lights in Wyre Street (right); the Cross Keys pub is on the left.

New estates generate windswept shopping precincts, 1970. Above: Greenstead; below: St John's. This enormous increase in the population tended to enhance town centre shopping, while the precincts on the estates struggled to survive.

Cars need car parks. Above: these houses in Priory Street were demolished in 1963, for 'temporary' car parking. (8T) Below: 'trust the motorist' in the Dutch Quarter, a scheme that was soon abandoned.

Vans clog the exit from Short Wyre Street. Servicing these town-centre shops presented many problems.

A surface car park outside the public library, 1973, is scheduled to become a 'town square'. (OP 151)

These weavers' cottages, seen in North Street in 1967, can represent the 500 small domestic properties that were demolished in redevelopments after 1965.

Eld Lane's Lady D'Arcy Almshouses were demolished in 1963. The one on the far left is now a shop.

Finch's Almshouses in St Nicholas Square were demolished by the Lion Walk development. They are now relocated in the Riverside Estate.

These we have lost. The Culver Street Methodist Church was demolished (above) and relocated as Castle Methodist Church. The Borough Electricity Works (below) in Osborne Street are also no longer standing. (12B)

The former Empire Cinema and Locke's garage (above) were removed for St Botolph's roundabout. (OP 126) This historic silk mill, built in 1826 and later a brewery store, grocery warehouse and plastics factory, was demolished in 1967 to make way for tower blocks behind St Peter's Street. The cottage, right, survives. (OP 34)

Stanwell Street (above) seen from Lion Walk church spire in 1969 and (below) at ground level, was largely destroyed by the building of Southway. Note 'Turner's' clothing factory, properly called The Colchester Manufacturing Company. (43B)

Culver Street was sliced in two by the Lion Walk development. The junction with Lion Walk has gone (seen above in 1972) as have the period buildings (seen below in 1967). What happened to the historic fire mark on the wall?

A last view (above) of St Botolph's Corner before the roundabout was built. (76T) Essex Street and the Essex Arms (seen below in 1967) were demolished for Southway.

An inelegant corner of Culver Street, now leading into the Lion Walk complex.

Centurion House in St John's Street was an early development by the property developers, Frincon, replacing an assortment of small period buildings. It is seen here in phase two of its construction in 1966. (8B)

Here and on the page opposite we gain some idea of the 'hole in the ground' created by the joint Frincon/Borough Lion Walk development, pictured here in 1974.

Tesco's shop window in High Street in 1965 still employs 'barrow-boy' advertising.

Lion Walk church dominates this half of the developers' crater. To its right a hole is being punched through the Roman Wall.

Colchester's first Chinese restaurant, 'The Rice Bowl', was later demolished for access to Culver Precinct.

Police help pedestrians across the St Botolph's Corner site in 1974, flooded when a mechanical digger ruptured a water main. Matters were made worse by digging an underpass on the site of an active medieval spring.

The Lion Walk development climbs skyward in 1975. St Botolph's roundabout is at the top right. (74,75)

The bus station multi-storey car park in 1977. This was eventually demolished because of structural faults.

Bricks are no longer made at Everett's Land Lane brickworks (left). Cement being mixed for new shops in Culver Street East, 1975 (right). (71B)

The Woolworths fire of 1973 brought the town to a standstill and a new, red-brick Woolworths to the High Street. (57T)

Fire destroyed this Crouch Street wine bar. It was reborn as a retirement home in 1986 with a marked reduction in decibels.

Anxious moments among the great and good of Colchester at the launch of the Civic Society in June 1964. Left to right: John Bensusan-Butt, Hervey Benham, Peter Russell Walker (back), Ivor Brown (hidden), Geoffrey Bone, F.S. Clayter. At the rear (among others) are Tony Doncaster and Bernard Mason.

The Civic Society's worst fears were realised with the destruction of the Regency assembly room at the Cups Hotel in 1968.

The giant telephone exchange 'tower' rises above the Dutch Quarter in 1969, built under crown immunity despite the Borough's opposition. Below is the skyline from Castle Park: to the left is the town hall, in the centre the BT Tower, and to the right St Peter's Church.

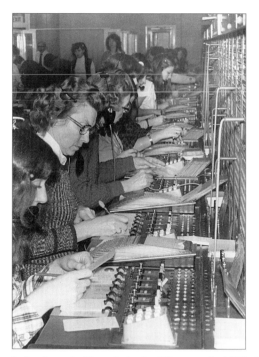 

Left: the switchboards in the BT tower in 1979. Right: the same place in 1984 and computers have arrived. By 1990, microchip technology cast doubt on the need to build the tower in the first place.

The approach to Vineyard Street car park in 1967: old houses still stand on the Roman Wall and billboards address the cars as they arrive.

These High Street façades were saved by planning control. Retail units in 1967, however, still cut across the boundaries of older buildings.

Cars block the top of Balkerne Hill, making the north–south journey across Colchester in 1968. (40T)

Balkerne Hill as it used to be, on a quiet day in 1969.

The Balkerne Hill dual carriageway under construction in 1976.

By 1988 the Balkerne Hill 'motorway' had bred a new urban geography. It was flanked by the St Mary's car park, with the Royal London and Anglia Water complexes one end and office property ringing the Maldon Road roundabout at the other. (104,105,109T)

Colchester became famous for roundabout experiments. In 1979 the East Street/Ipswich Road junction needed three policemen to explain it (above). In 1972 the Albert roundabout was made from car tyres (below). (28T)

Hythe Level Crossing is still manually controlled and used by cyclists more than juggernauts in this pre-1960 photograph.

Colchester North Station was electrified in 1969. The travel time to London became less than an hour and the ranks of commuters swelled. (37T) (OP 40B)

The last train leaves as 'Beeching's Axe' closes the Brightlingsea line, eleven years after the 1953 floods had swept it away. (37B)

More floods at Wivenhoe in 1965, recalling the terrible North Sea surge of 1953.

Flooding at the Hythe while it is still a prosperous port. Note the large grain elevator overshadowing the historic maltings and the distant New Quay bonded warehouse.

The opening of the new Hythe Sewage Works in 1971. It was still being accused of making bad smells in 1990. (OP 23B)

The old livestock market, Middleborough, 1964, eleven years before it moved to Severalls Lane. (OP 20T)

Sheep being auctioned in 1968. The crane in the background is associated with the building works in St Peter's Street. (105T)

The High Street market survives: in 1955 (left) and in 1982 (right).

The market during a spell in Culver Street East in 1968. (OP 135T)

The signs of cultural change. The High Steward, Lord Alport, and workmen toast the new Mercury Theatre rising up behind them in 1971.

The last night at the Repertory Theatre, Albert Hall in 1972. Left: manager David Forder and the cast take a bow. Right: the audience sing 'Auld Lang Syne', Lady Alport is at the front on the left.

The hushed somnolence of the old Borough Reference Library. As was so often at this date, it is not overcrowded. (OP 151)

The Cameo Arts Cinema, in St John's Street, 1976, offered 'alternative' cinema – part classical and part risqué.

The launch of Colchester's first evening paper, the *Evening Gazette* in 1970. Left: the telex provides national news. Right: the revolutionary web offset printworks at QB in Sheepen Road. Below: Mervyn Donnelly, sales director, with one of the 'drop-off Mums' who organized the 500 delivery boys and girls.

Pupils stroll from the Philip Morant School, one of seven postwar secondary schools built in Colchester. Each school eventually developed its own sixth form. (123B)

Friars Grove Junior School, 1973. This scene vividly illustrates the pupil-centred learning of the day. (OP 119)

Above: the massive University of Essex campus under construction in 1966. Below: student unrest in 1977. Sir Keith Joseph (standing), Conservative Party policy spokesman, takes on student hecklers in front of the media, which led the *Sunday Times* to call for the university's closure.

Antony Buck, hoisted on high by young Conservatives on the night of his 1970 election victory, was a Colchester MP for over thirty-two years.

Matt Saunders, one of the first eighteen-year-old voters, votes on his eighteenth birthday at Alderman Blaxill School polling station at the October 1974 General Election.

The former Headgate Chapel, now relocated at Ireton Road, became the Labour Club in 1977 (and later the Warehouse Restaurant). (OP 63B)

The opening of St Edmund's Hall in 1966, an Anglican church and community centre to serve the vast new Greenstead Estate.

A rare 1971 picture of the old borough council in session before the new district council was set up in 1974. The Mayor is Nancy 'The Hat' Smith, so nicknamed for her penchant for impressive headgear. She is flanked by Richard Wheeler, Deputy Mayor and Norman Catchpole, Town Clerk.

Opening the Oyster Fishery in 1969 – a fine old civic ritual. Mayor Reg Hilham is assisted by Hervey Benham (left), masquerading as a deck hand, Jim Spong (Town Sergeant) and Norman Catchpole (Town Clerk). (OP 114)

The 'decision makers' meet at the Braiswick golf club, Borough v. Army, May 1971. Left to right: Don Harrison, Chairman of Planning, General Jack Dye, Garrison Commander, Richard Wheeler, Mayor, two army officers and Mike Green, Borough Engineer.

Princess Anne opens the Youth House (now the Town House) in Stockwell Street, 1969.

King Coel's Kittens, outstanding charity fund-raisers, decorate a car for the 1963 Severalls Fête. This photograph shows Ian McMeekan and David Snow in Culver Street car park. (13B,65B)

A tiddlywinks race in Culver Street organized by King Coel's Kittens in the late 1960s. This was in the early days of such 'sponsored larks'.

Journalist Bill Tucker entertains the fifty-one entrants for the 1971 Carnival Queen contest. The winner was Antoinette Jenkins, who is on the far right.

The 1971 Carnival progresses down the High Street, led by a military band.

The old outdoor bathing pool on a summer's day in 1972. (120T) It was converted into a boating lake when the dual carriageway link was built to North Station Road.

A full house at Layer Road for Colchester United's famous victory over Leeds United in February 1971. This photograph shows a rare attack on the Leeds goal with Jack Charlton, centre right. (OP 154)

1977–1990
GROUNDS
FOR OPTIMISM

(John Cobley, Town Clerk)

The out-of-town Tollgate Centre offers modern motor car shopping, but by 1990 had not realized its plans for a drive-in cinema.

From the air the fortress-like Royal London Headquarters dominates Middleborough in 1984. Old red roofs line North Hill, travelling diagonally across the picture, but the BT tower and the car park behind Williams & Griffins overshadow the Dutch Quarter.

The clearance of the Royal London site, in 1979, produced exciting rescue archaeology: crowds gather to view an elaborate Roman mosaic, now displayed in the Castle Museum. (89B)

The Royal London HQ, rising to completion in 1982, dominates a small barber's shop, the only survivor of an historic street line. (104)

A lorry with a hawser removes the roof from the old Drill Hall in 1984, where Baden-Powell entertained the town and police boxing teams performed.

A large crater fills up with the long-awaited Culver Precinct in 1985, complete with underground delivery access.

An officious ban on photography in the new Culver Square prompted the rebellious press to shoot an amused model, 1989. (65B)

Culver Precinct entertainment included a male voice choir from Colchester's German twin town Wetzlar in 1988.

Supermarkets abound. Above: Sainsbury's store at Lexden, 1983, before they moved to Tollgate. Below: Tesco's in St John's Street, 1986, before it was sold and acquired Greek porticos.

Multi-storey car parks abound. Above: the castellated St Mary's on the Balkerne Motorway in 1981. Below: the honest core of Stanwell Street, 1990, before it acquired Legoland bricks and pediments. (20, 83)

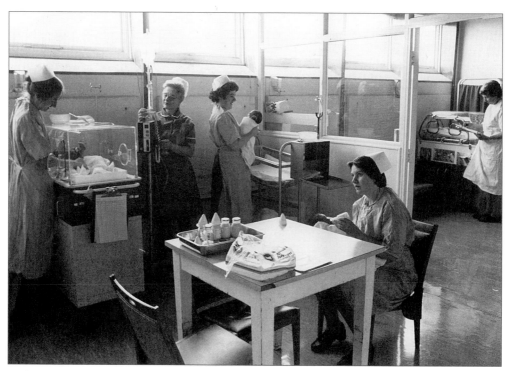

Medical Colchester. Above: the new Special Care Unit at the Maternity Hospital on Lexden Road, 1979. Below: mealtime at Essex Hall, 1977, a Victorian institution that closed in the 1980s. (28T, OP 65)

Colchester's new Queen Elizabeth District Hospital, 1983, with High Woods beyond and Turner Village beside it.

St Helena Hospice Day Centre, funded entirely by Robin Tomkins (right) of Frincon Holdings, seen here with the mayor and mayoress, John and Mamie Lampon, in 1987.

High-tech production line at Trebor's modern factory in Severalls Lane Business Park, 1986.

Cars quietly graze outside the Peartree Road Business Units, each carefully numbered in case they get confused, 1987.

New housing at High Woods, 1983, a vast improvement on the Orlitt units of 1947. (30T)

The temple of commerce: High Woods Tesco store under construction amidst the trees, 1981. (108B)

An industrial dispute at Ozalid in 1980. This firm was the unhappy successor to Bernard Mason's office equipment empire and went through eleven managing directors in three years, before becoming the core of the Cowdray Centre for small businesses. (OP 133)

Colchester Lathe Company, 1975. This is the main machine shop with programme control milling machines; the firm, which dramatically closed in 1992, still had a workforce of over 1,000 staff at this date.

Paxmans survived with a reduced workforce and consolidated plant. Britannia Works were demolished (seen below in 1987), but in that same year the firm completed orders for the 5,000 b.h.p. Valenta marine engine (above). An Admiralty team, led by Rear Admiral Sherval, is seen with managing director, Jack Fryer and senior Paxman staff.

Midland Bank's new computer room in the High Street, seen here in 1979, provides, like the Royal London, new office-based employment. (58B, 81T, 104)

Men search the new Job Centre (left) in High Street, 1978. Women assemble motors for industrial fans at Woods of Colchester, 1984 (right). (OP 100B, OP 153T)

This corner shop survives at Canterbury Road in 1986, by dint of long hours and loyal customers.

Tentative efforts to promote tourism include open-top bus tours, beginning at the Castle in 1990. (OP 57)

The Jehovah's Witnesses built a new church off Elmstead Road in just two days in 1984.

A familiar sight in Colchester for over 100 years: the Salvation Army march down Head Street past the site of the Fleece Hotel in 1982. (OP 121T, OP 158)

Plain-clothes police remove goods from Colchester's 'sex shop' in Butt Road, 1981.

Police confront drinkers at the 'new' Cups Hotel in Trinity Street, 1982, after complaints about the overflow into Holy Trinity churchyard. By 1990 the churchyard railings, removed in the war, had been restored. (11T)

'Old hardy annual': the Colchester Rose Show, 1986. Bob Russell, Colchester's first Social Democrat mayor, presents the Luther Russell Cup, named after his grandfather, to Angus Caution.

'New hardy annual': the Fireswim, in Colchester's new indoor pool, 1983, became a big charity event. In the centre, Antony Buck MP takes a dive. (102T)

The bi-annual Colchester Tattoo, a joint town and garrison venture, grew to become the largest in Britain. Until 1984 it was held in Castle Park. Here teams of boys prepare for the traditional dismantling and carrying of a gun carriage across a divide (47T).

Left: During Castle restoration a sycamore tree, believed to have been planted to celebrate the defeat of Napoleon, is preserved in its own giant pot, 1987. (OP 57) Right: teenagers muster for a visit to the new Debenhams Store of soap star, Jason Donovan, 1988.

Left: St Botolph's Church became a notable centre for live music, 1982. (OP 141T) Right: Rollerworld at East Bay makes Colchester the roller-skating capital of Britain, 1990.

Re-using theatres. Left, EMI Bingo in the Playhouse, St John's Street, 1983. Right: the opening night at the Hippodrome, 1988, reborn as a night club (28B).

Pupils at Gilberd School march in protest against a proposed Sixth Form College at the Gilberd School site, 1980. In the event, the Sixth Form College proved to be a great success. (OP 153B)

A traffic jam on Ipswich Road's approach to Cowdray Avenue – note the Colchester roundabout. In 1989, people walk less . . .

. . . but run more. The massed start of the 1984 Colchester Fun Run, a symbol of active leisure and the elusive goal of universal health and happiness.

On 31 December 1990 a queue gathers for the closing-down sale of Evans the Ironmonger on North Hill:
another old family business gone.

ACKNOWLEDGEMENTS

Thanks are due to the following for the use of photographs:
Essex County Newspapers pp. 36T, 39, 40T, 48B, 52, 53T, 55, 58B, 59, 60, 62B, 63, 65B, 71B, 72T, 73–75, 77T, 78, 81T, 83B, 84–86, 88–94, 97, 98, 102T, 103, 104, 105B, 107–120, 122–126; Colchester Museums pp. 7–19, 38, 50T; K. Mirams pp. 36B, 43B, 67T, 68, 69, 70T, 72B, 79B, 80, 81B, 82T; Colchester District Council pp. 40B, 65T, 77B; Colchester & East Essex Co-op Society p. 51; J. Sainsbury plc p. 61; B. Polley pp. 2, 23, 37T, 42, 45B, 62T, 71T, 82B; J. Robinson p. 24; G. Bober pp. 29T, 53B, 64, 69B, 70B; M. Glover pp. 29B, 76T, 101B; J. Wright pp. 34B, 37B, 56, 57B; C. Mabbitt pp. 47T, 79T; D. Woodward pp. 66B, 67, 96B; University of Essex p. 95; North Essex Conservative Association 96T; J. Bensusan-Butt 101T; King Coel's Kittens pp. 100, 101T; Colchester Archaeological Trust 105T; Rollerworld 122B.

BRITAIN IN OLD PHOTOGRAPHS

To order any of these titles please telephone our distributor, Littlehampton Book Services on 01903 721596
For a catalogue of these and our other titles please ring Regina Schinner on 01453 731114